Salvo Spedale

HOW TO MATCH FOOD AND WINE

Practical manual to learn step by step the techniques of food-wine matching

Assovini.it

PRESENTATION

The beautiful journey towards the perfect matching of food and wine begins with the discovery of the perfumes and the typical flavours of the territories in which only in those territories they manage to express the maximum gustative pleasure.

Simple or sophisticated specialities find in the wine their ideal company, capable of well enhancing their merits and, sometimes, capable of revealing a hidden quality or toning down the most ardent tones.

The wine-food matching, subject of heated exchanges among important wine and food lovers, is one of the favourite subject among people from all classes; people talk about it everywhere: in fashionable saloons, in web forums, in TV broadcasts and in the pages of newspapers and magazines of every order and degree.

Magical symbiosis between the flavours of wine and food, their matching cannot be handled with superficiality or reduced at a simple list of specialities and wines, proposed building only on experience or the improvisation of the moment, with the desire of amazing.
At the contrary, it must be the result of repeated tastes and samples, crossed with every variant, until the application of a precise technique to evaluate the harmony.

Simple and linear, this manual gives the instruments to approach the world of wine-food matching from the main door, interpreting the sensations and speaking about them with a synthetic but exhaustive and effective language. It will be the personal experience, the passion and the deepening that allows to become expert and competent tasters.

Salvo Spedale
President of Assovini
Director of Panel Assovini Sommelier
Sommelier AIS

ASSOVINI (National Association of Wine Producers and Wine Tourism)
www.assovini.it - The Portal of Wine and Wineries
www.assovini.com - The 1° didactic E-commerce of Wine

INDICE

SENSORIAL ANALYSIS OF FOOD

- **Visual exam – introduction**
  - Aspect
  - Presentation

- **Olfactive exam – introduction**
  - Franckness
  - Olfactive harmony
  - Olfactive quality

- **Taste-olfactive exam – introduction**
  - Perceptibility degree
  - Perceptibility sensations
  - Structure

- **Taste-olfactive balance**

- **Overall harmony**

SENSORIAL ANALISYS OF WINE

- **Olfactive exam**

- **Taste-olfactive persistence**

- **Taste-olfactive exam**

AIS METHOD OF WINE-FOOD MATCHING

- **Principle of contraposition**

- **Principle of concordance**

- **Examples of wine-food matching**

SENSORIAL ANALISYS OF FOOD

The sensorial analysis of food, useful to the food-wine matching, is made up of thre steps, that are the visual, olfactive and gustative exams.

VISUAL EXAM – INTRODUCTION

First of all it's important to consider the psychological effect that the food/preparation can produce in those who are about to consume a meal, because it can stimulate him both mentally and physiologically.
The observation of the meal allows also to evaluate the integrity state in terms of hygiene and food safety.
The visual exam tries to evaluate the aspect and the presentation of the food/preparation in order to express a properly judgement.

1. ASPECT

It's referred to its state of integrity and freshness.

- **Not very pleasant.** When its external characteristics are pretty different from those that represent its optimal state of freshness, that often indicate its best organoleptic characteristics.

- **Acceptable.** When its external characteristics aren't much different from those that represent its optimal state of freshness and integrity.

- **Inviting.** When its external characteristics are exactly those that represents its optimal state of freshness and alimentary integrity.

2. PRESENTATION

It's the principle on which the philosophy of certain type of cuisine is based. A good presentation can enhance every preparation.

- **Not very pleasant**. When the disposition of the various components of the meal is disordered, casual, without any particular attention at the chromatic combination or possible particular shapes.

- **Acceptable.** When the disposition of the various components of the meal is ordered and not casual, but without any attention at the chromatic combination or possible particular shapes.

- **Inviting.** When the disposition of the various components of the meal is ordered and there is a certain care in the chromatic combination and in the geometry of their disposition.

OLFACTIVE EXAM

The exam is performed through a precise evaluation of the perfumes that are perceptible in the moment in which the meal is served.
It's obviously important that the perfumes of the preparation are perceived in a "comparable way" with the perfumes of the paired wine, in order to avoid a prevalence of the characteristics of one on each other.

The serving temperature of a food/preparation is fundamental for its olfactive evaluation, because the molecules that are responsible of the perfumes are less volatile in a cold meal, so they have less probabilities in impressing the cells of the olfactory mucosa. Through the olfactive exam we propose to evaluate, in particular, the frankness, the olfactive harmony and the olfactive quality of the food/preparation.

1. FRANKNESS

It's the set of the olfactive characteristics of the tasted food, that allows to recognize the typicity of the product, that are its organoleptic characteristics.

- **Not very pleasant.** When the olfactive sensations are flattened and not very characteristic of the examined product.

- **Acceptable.** When it's possible to recognize what we're tasting even if the olfactive sensations aren't very characteristic of the examined product.

- **Inviting.** When it's possible to recognize in a clearly and definitive way what we're tasting, because the olfactive characteristics are strong and unmistakable, very characteristic of the examined product.

2. OLFACTIVE HARMONY

It represents the perfect fusion of the perfumes of a certain preparation, expressed in a proportioned balance, without any false notes and without any of them prevailing on each other in a strong way.

- **Not very pleasant.** When the set of the perfumes isn't amalgamated and presents obvious false notes due to the predominance of one or some of them.

- **Acceptable.** When the set of the perfumes is quite amalgamated, without any strong predominance of one so some of them, but the combination results being quite pleasant.

- **Inviting.** When the set of the perfumes is perfectly amalgamated, without any predominance of one on each other.

3. OLFACTIVE QUALITY

It's the synthesis of the judgement that is expressed according to the olfactive characteristics of a food/preparation and it's the result of the single evaluations especially related to the frankness and/or the harmony. It represents a quite subjective aspect in the food tasting.

- **Not very pleasant.** When the perfume of the food/preparation results being poor and mediocre. The frankness is often covered or there is a dispersion of the initially present perfumes or a deterioration of them due to a bad preparation and/or conservation.

- **Acceptable.** When the perfume of the food/preparation is sufficiently fine and pleasant, with a own properly frankness if referred to the single aliment and with a good harmony in which every perfume can be perceived in a pleasant way.

- **Inviting.** When the perfume of the food/preparation is balanced and frank, full of perfectly amalgamated scents, capable to impress our olfaction in a favourably way.

TASTE-OLFACTIVE EXAM

It's the most important moment in the food tasting, fundamental in the choice of the most properly wine.

Through the gustative exam we propose to evaluate all the organoleptic characteristics. They are determined by the four fundamental flavours (sweet, bitter, acid, salty), by the cooking liquids and by every dressing eventually added (oils, greases, aromatic herbs and spices), as well as their structure.

So it's necessary analysing the gustative and taste-olfactive sensations, like sapidity, bitter tendency, acid tendency, sweetness, sweet tendency, spicing, aromaticity and the taste-olfactory persistence, as well as tactile sensations like oiliness, succulence and greasiness.

- **Sapidity**
- **Bitter tendency**
- **Acid tendency**
- **Sweetness**
- **Spiciness**
- **Aromaticity**
- **Oiliness**
- **Succulence**
- **Sweet tendency**
- **Greasiness**
- **Taste-olfactory persistence**

DEGREE OF PERCEPTIBILITY

- **Imperceptible (0-1-2).** A gustative or taste-olfactive sensation can be called "imperceptible if there is no way to perceive it or if it's just a hint.

- **Not very perceptible (2-3-4).** A gustative or taste-olfactory can be called "not very perceptible" if it's possible to perceive it in a recognizable way, but also in this case, it's not defined.

- **Quite perceptible (4-5-6).** A gustative or taste-olfactive sensation can be called "quite perceptible" if it's possible to sufficiently identify and perceive it. It's a quantitative evaluation and not a judge over the pleasantness.

- **Perceptible (6-7-8).** A gustative or taste-olfactive sensation can be called "perceptible" if it's possible to identify and perceive it in a clearly way and the stimulus is very defined.

- **Very perceptible (8-9-10).** A gustative or taste-olfactive sensation can be defined "very perceptible" if it's possible to identify and perceive it in a clearly way and that's the one that allows to identify a meal or characterize a more complex preparation.

After evaluating all the mentioned sensations, we can express a judgement about the structure of the food/preparation. (synthesis characteristic).

Only after the analysis of all the gustative and tactile characteristics and their evaluation in terms of perceptibility, it will be possible to express a judgement about its gustative balance, because every ingredient must be perfectly integrated with the others.

At the end of the gustative exam, considering the evaluation that is expressed for every organoleptic characteristic that is analysed during the three steps of the sensorial analysis, it will be possible to express the final judgement about the overall harmony of the proposed food/preparation.

TASTE-OLFACTORY SENSATIONS

SAPIDITY. The sapidity is one of the four fundamental gustative sensations, especially perceived by the fungiform papillae present in the rear side and dorsal zones of the tongue. The principal flavour that is referred at the term "sapidity" is the "salty" and so it's easy to attribute the perceptibility of this sensation at the presence of salt or salt derivatives in foods/preparations.
The salt can be present inside the food (for example in cured meats such as coppa, lard, salami bacon; Cheeses such as pecorino and grana in which the sapidity increases directly in proportion to the seasoning time).
Other foods in which the sensation of sapidity is perceptible are fish such as herring, cod, stockfish, in which it is the particular preparation technique that determines an increase in the salt content.
Salt can also be added in more or less abundant quantities as a condiment in different preparations.
The flavour of a preparation is determined, in addition to the normal cooking salt, also with monosodium glutamate (base of common nuts).

BITTER TENDENCY. The bitter tendency is one of the four fundamental gustative sensations, perceived in particular by the goblet papillae present in the back area of the tongue.
It's necessary to talk of "bitter tendency" and not "bitter feeling" because it's unlikely to find a "really bitter" food / preparation, and this would also be an unpleasant characteristic and would not make any harmonious combination possible. The bitter tendency is characteristic of all the grilled preparations, whether they are based on fish products, meats, cheeses and vegetables, since this type of cooking causes the formation of slightly carbonized substances on the surface of the food, responsible for this sensation.
Even an excessive addition of spices and aromatic herbs, above all, prolonged cooking in the presence of these, can determine this sensation.
It's necessary to remember that there are foods that provide bitter tendencies for their intrinsic qualities. Among these are Treviso radicchio, artichoke, chicory, raw spinach; foods of animal origin such as liver, or confectionery preparations such as those based on dark chocolate, capable of determining this sensation at an appreciable level of perceptibility.

ACID TENDENCY. The acid tendency is one of the four fundamental gustative sensations, perceived in particular by the fungiform papillae present in the anterior areas of the tongue and sub-lingual.
It is necessary to speak only of acid tendency and not of actual acidity, because this would result in a too accentuated characteristic of food / preparation, to allow a harmonious combination.
And this is why some foods / preparations, such as citrus fruits or salads seasoned with plenty of vinegar, are not offered with any wine.
What has been observed so far also leads to advise against the indiscriminate addition of lemon juice on many preparations, as is sometimes done with some fish, meats and cured meats, because it interferes with the original flavours of the meal.
The foods in which the sensation of acid tendency is perceptible are above all

those based on tomato sauce and those that have been marinated in vinegar or lemon.
Vinegar in abundant quantity is the enemy of wine. However, there is an exception, represented by the traditional balsamic vinegar.
In this particular product the acidic notes are made less aggressive and almost velvety by the sweet, aromatic and soft components that derive from the care in processing and long aging. But also the combination of preparations with traditional balsamic vinegar is not the easiest, because it requires wines of good structure, mature or aged, with a great softness and a particularly complex bouquet.

SWEETNESS. Sweetness is one of the four fundamental gustative sensations, perceived in particular by the fungiform papillae present on the tip of the tongue. The perception of this sensation is determined by the presence in foods of simple sugars, monosaccharides such as fructose present above all in fruit, glucose, galactose, or disaccharides such as sucrose, the normal sugar used and the lactose that is present in milk. It's a sensation always linked to real confectionery preparations, such as creams, puddings, cakes, pastries, biscuits, even if the degree of perceptibility of their sweetness can be very different.
But in addition to the actual presence of different amounts of sugar, the perception of the sensation of sweetness is conditioned by the ingredients that are present (eg cocoa, fruit, jam, cream that are used for filling).

SPICINESS. The spicy sensation is linked to the presence of spices in the food / preparation, which can be used both individually and combined together, characterizing it in a decidedly recognizable way.
This sensation can sometimes be accompanied by a "spicy" flavor, more or less accentuated, pungent, in some cases almost irritating to the oral mucosa, while in other cases it may fade into a bitter tendency, especially if the spices are subjected to long cooking.
The feeling of spiciness can therefore be perceived differently depending on the type and quantity of spices used.
Foods characterized by these spicy sensations are the cured meats, as for example. the speck, the coppa piacentina, the bacon, the mortadella, the Tuscan and Calabrese salami and some aged cheeses, for which both the addition of spices during the production phases and the seasoning are decisive.
As regards the preparations in which the spicy sensation is perceptible, we can remember first courses such as the classic Milanese risotto due to the presence of saffron, several seconds with curry-based sauces, peppery preparations in general (pepper fillet, salmì made with game), up to desserts (strudel, panforte).

AROMATICITY. The aromatic sensation is easily recognizable, since it is linked to the presence above all of aromatic herbs in the food/preparation, which can also be used in different combinations and proportions between them.
The feeling is generally less aggressive, more delicate and pleasant than that due to spiciness, but it can be equally perceptible depending on the type of aromatic herb, its state of preservation, whether fresh or dried and the quantity used.
Among the foods we can mention some cheeses (blue cheeses such as gorgonzola, mature pecorino cheeses), cured meats (speck and other smoked, Mantua salami

with garlic, Tuscan finocchiona).
The aromatic herbs are added in many preparation (oregano in the caprese, chives in the green salad, basil in the pesto, parsley in the green sauce, bay laurel in the roasts, tarragon for the fillet, thyme for the roast lamb and dill for the salmon).
Some desserts offer perceptible sensations of aroma due to the addition of coffee, such as tiramisu, or liqueurs such as crepe suzette.

OILINESS. The oiliness is a tactile sensation, perceived on the tongue, on the oral mucosa placed on the sides of the mouth and on the palate.
It's perceived with a sense of "slipperiness" in the mouth, linked to the presence of an oily and non-aqueous component and therefore with a different "consistency".
The oiliness of a food or a preparation is determined by the presence above all of oils, fluid fats of vegetable origin, produced both from olives and from seeds of different types.
Extra virgin olive oils have different fluidity and seed oils, in general, are more fluid than olive oils. With the same amount of oil used, different sensations of oiliness are perceived.
The level of perceptibility of greasiness in similar preparations and other conditions being equal, can vary depending on even a small amount of another ingredient.
The sensation of greasiness can also be perceived in preparations in which solid fats present in the ingredients, following the high cooking temperature, melt and trasform into a fluid state (like braised meats, pork ribs, sausages).

SUCCULENCE.

The succulence is a tactile sensation, perceived inside the oral cavity, limited to the presence of liquids in the mouth. First of all, we can talk about intrinsic food/preparation succulence, necessary for the presence, within the same, of juices that are easily released during chewing (for example cooked meat served hot).
Succulence is also due to the addition of liquids during preparation or during cooking (for example braised meats, stews, stews, fish soups and the like, in which succulence is due to wine, tomato sauce, broth or another liquid in which the food is cooked even for very long times).
The induced succulence is instead determined by foods/preparations that cause abundant salivation during chewing and even after swallowing. The foods/preparations responsible for this phenomenon are not particularly rich in internal juices and therefore have the "need" to produce saliva, necessary for their imbibition and subsequent swallowing.
All foods are capable of causing induced succulence, albeit at very different levels of perceptibility.
Some foods that have been marinated with wine, vinegar or lemon are characterized by succulence due to the addition of liquids, but are also able to cause induced succulence.

SWEET TENDENCY. The sweet tendency is a gustative sensation pleasantly perceived in the mouth, but not comparable with the clear and decisive perceptibility of the sensation of sweetness. It is therefore a more nuanced and delicate, but equally recognizable sensation.

Among the foods of vegetal origin that can determine a clear sensation of sweet tendency are carrots, squash, some types of onions that contain small amounts of simple sugars; starch-based foods such as cereals, rice, pasta, bread; legumes such as peas and beans; vegetables like potatoes.
Among the foods of animal origin that can make this sensation be perceived are crustaceans, horsemeat, all the meats cooked in blood and some sausages such as sausage and ham (these cured meats contain oil that often contributes to accentuating the feeling of sweet tendency).

GREASINESS. The greasiness is a tactile sensation especially perceived on the tongue, but also on the oral mucosa placed on the sides of the mouth and palate. This sensation is perceived with a sense of "furred" on the surface of the tongue and of "softness" throughout the oral cavity.
The greasiness of a food/preparation is due to the presence of solid fats and therefore especially of animal origin, such as lard, cured meats, many cheeses or egg yolk.
The greasiness of a food tends to "knead" the mouth and, sometimes, in foods such as pig's trotters and sausages, to determine almost a feeling of "stickiness", due however above all to the presence of connective tissue (collagen).
The perceptibility of the sensation of greasiness depends on the amount of oils present, on the other possible components of the preparation, and on the structure of the food itself.
The butter is an oil that has a solid consistency at ambient temperature and therefore should cause a distinct sensation of greasiness. It is often used in the molten state and therefore assumes its own definite fluidity, perceived in the mouth especially as greasiness.
Solid oils almost always accentuate the feeling of sweet tendency.

TASTE-OLFACTIVE PERSISTENCE. The taste-olfactive persistence of a food / preparation is a sensation due to the permanence, inside the oral cavity, of the gustative and tactile sensations just described, as well as of those olfactory retronasal sensations that can be perceived after swallowing.
It's therefore a sensorial characteristic comparable to the **intense aromatic persistence (I.A.P.)** considered during the wine tasting. Each food has its own taste-olfactory persistence, depending on the different components present and the type of cooking applied.

STRUCTURE

The structure of a food/preparation is determined by its composition, the type and quantity (number) of the ingredients, which determine a greater or lesser complexity of taste, besides a different consistency. A similar sensation, determined by the paired wine, must correspond to it.

According to the structure, a meal can be defined as:

- **Not very structured** , if it has been prepared with a limited number of ingredients, characterized by slightly accentuated taste sensations, possibly determined also by cooking that does not particularly enrich the preparation (white rice seasoned with only butter or extra virgin olive oil, first courses seasoned with delicate sauces based on vegetables, molluscs or crustaceans, white meats without any elaborate sauce, lean steamed or boiled fish served only with extra virgin olive oil, some leavened desserts such as pandoro or torta paradiso).

- **Quite structured**, if it has a certain gustatory complexity, due both to the ingredients used and to the type of preparation or cooking to which it has been subjected (first courses seasoned with sauces enriched by the aromas of aromatic herbs, from cream, parmesan and salted butter, to main courses such as white or red meat roasts, baked fish or served with simple sauces, desserts such as pastries, jam and fruit tarts, panettone and homemade donuts).

- **Structured,** if it presents a wide and articulated gustatory complexity, due to ingredients and condiments such as oils and sauces, as well as spices and aromatic herbs, able to characterize in a decisive way the preparation, which presents strong and diversified flavours (first courses like tortellini, agnolotti with ragout) of meat, baked lasagna, some risottos like the one with the sausage, roasted harness with pancetta, stews, braised meat, jugged hare and other game-based preparations, desserts based on chocolate or shortcrust pastry with elaborate creams and fillings others like the panforte, the torrone and the croccante).

GUSTATIVE BALANCE

The gustative balance of a food / preparation is determined by the set of perceived sensations that should be such as not to determine some clear predominance of one over the others, always considering the characteristics of each product and the different ingredients.

Similarly to what is considered in the gustatory analysis of wine, even in foods we can find taste sensations that can be traced back to the concept of softness (fatness and sweetness) and hardness (flavour and acidity).
Also in this case they will have to be present in such a way that none is so relevant as to dominate the others.

According to the balance, a food/preparation can be defined as:

- **Unbalanced.** In the case that one or more components or ingredients stand out in a particular and unpleasant way during the gustatory examination.

- **Quite balanced.** In the case that no component or ingredient stands out excessively from the others, even if one perceives a certain predominance of one of them.

- **Balanced.** In the case that no component or ingredient stands out in a particular way compared to the others, thus creating a correct and pleasant proportion between the different perceived gustative sensations.

OVERALL HARMONY

It means expressing a judgment that considers all the characteristics evaluated during the visual, olfactive and gustatory examination, summarizing everything that has impressed us in a positive and negative sense in order to assess the globality of the food examined.
The overall harmony therefore represents the synthesis of the sensorial analysis and must express a perfect agreement between the different components, which must be in a pleasant proportion so that a positive judgment can be expressed.

According to the overall harmony, a food/preparation can be defined as:

- **Not very harmonious.** When there is a marked discrepancy between the components responsible for the organoleptic characteristics, evaluated above all at the olfactive and gustative level, without neglecting the appearance and presentation.

- **Quite harmonious.** When there is some slight imperfection in one or more components responsible for the organoleptic characteristics, evaluated above all at the olfactive and gustative level, without neglecting the appearance and presentation.

- **Harmonious.** When all the components responsible for the organoleptic characteristics, evaluated above all at the olfactive and gustative level, combine perfectly and also the appearance and presentation are inviting.

SENSORIAL ANALYSIS OF WINE

INTRODUCTION

The sensorial analysis of wine for the purpose of combining food and wine is the second step that must be taken to be able to achieve a harmonious combination with a food / preparation and to be able to judge whether the proposed one can be considered valid or, at contrary, present the prevalence of some characteristic of tho food or wine. Not all the features considered in the wine tasting are, at this stage, taken into consideration: in this case a detailed description of the colour or an evaluation of the fineness and of the composition of the wine bouquet appears superfluous.

The fundamental characteristics to be assessed during the taste-olfactory examination are the olfactory intensity and intense aromatic persistence (IAP), while during the gustative examination it's important to analyse and quantify the sweetness, softness, alcohol content, tannins, the effervescence, the flavour, the acidity and the structure or body of the wine, since they are those directly involved in achieving the best harmony between preparation and wine.

In fact, each of them will have to go against each other or, depending on the case, come to agreement, with each specific gustatory and taste-olfactory characteristic of the food/preparation, so that the combination is perfectly harmonious.

OLFACTIVE EXAM

OLFACTORY INTENSITY. It's the set of all fragrant sensations perceived in the wine, regardless of their different composition, complexity and evolution. It's a purely "quantitative" aspect of the wine aromas to match.

- **Deficient (0-2).** It's said of a wine in which very few odorous sensations occur, almost not to be perceived.

- **Not very intense (2-4).** It's said of a wine in which scented sensations are scarce, not very perceptible to the sense of smell.

- **Quite intense (4-6).** It's said of a wine in which the fragrant sensations are fairly perceptible, fine and delicate.

- **Intense (6-8).** It's said of a wine in which the scent sensations are well perceptible, often in a pronounced way.

- **Very intense (8-10).** It's said of a wine in which the odorous sensations are particularly perceptible, intense and enveloping.

TASTE-OLFACTIVE PERSISTENCE

The permanence of the gustatory, tactile and retro-nasal olfactory sensations that, after swallowing, are perceived by our senses in their complexity and totality.

- **Short.** It's said of a wine in which there is a taste-olfactive persistence of less than 2 seconds.

- **Not very persistent.** It's said of a wine in which there is a taste-olfactive persistence of 2-4 seconds.

- **Quite persistent.** It's said of a wine in which there is a taste-olfactive persistence of 4-6 seconds.

- **Persistent.** It's said of a wine in which there is a taste-olfactive persistence of 6-8 seconds.

- **Very persistent.** It's said of a wine in which there is a taste-olfactive persistence of more than 8 seconds.

TASTE-OLFACTIVE EXAM

It's the fundamental step of the sensorial analysis for pairing purposes.

EFFERVESCENCE. At the level of taste it influences both the sensations of hardness and softness, as it tends to accentuate the former (acidity, sapidity and tannins) and to dampen the latter (sweetness, pseudo-caloric sensation and softness).

According to the effervescence a wine can be defined as:

- **Still (0-2).** It is said of a wine that does not present any effervescence or it's present at an imperceptible level.

- **Not very effervescent (2-4).** It is said of a wine in which the effervescence is perceived in a recognizable way. Normally these are lively wines.

- **Quite effervescent (4-6).** It is said of a wine in which the effervescence is perceived in a "sufficient" way. Normally these are sparkling wines.

- **Effervescent (6-8).** It is said of a wine in which the effervescence is perceived in a marked way. Normally these are sparkling wines.

- **Very effervescent (8-10).** It is said of a wine in which the effervescence is perceived in a marked way. Normally these are sparkling wines in which carbon dioxide is present in greater quantities than the previous ones.

SWEETNESS

Sweetness is a gustative sensation that can be perceived distinctly on the tip of the tongue only in wines with a rather high sugar residue (generally in sweet sparkling wines, passito wines and in some liqueur wines).
If the quantity of sugar is very low, there is no real feeling of sweetness, but of softness.

According to the sweetness, a wine can be defined as:

- **Dry (0-2).** It is said of a wine in which the sensation of sweetness is not perceived, with a residual sugar between 1-5 g/litre, which contributes to determine a certain softness.

- **Semisweet (2-4).** It is said of a wine in which a very slight sensation of sweetness is perceived, with a residual sugar normally between 10-20 g/litre.

- **Lovely (4-6).** It is said of a wine in which a sensation of sweetness is clearly perceived, with a residual sugar normally between 20-50 g/litre.

- **Sweet (6-8).** It is said of a wine in which a sensation of sweetness is clearly perceived, with a residual sugar normally between 50-100 g/litre, or between 100-160 g/litre in some sweet and liqueur wines.

- **Fulsome (8-10).** It is said of a wine in which a strong and predominant sensation of sweetness is perceived, not well supported by the other components and therefore represents an anomalous situation.

ALCOHOLICITY

Alcohols present in wine, in particular ethyl alcohol, determine a tactile sensation inside the oral cavity due to their vasodilatory and dehydrating action.
As a result of this phenomenon, a more or less perceptible sensation of "pseudo-heat" is perceived, which manifests itself with an apparent sensation of "hot and dry" that is felt on the whole mucous membrane of the mouth.

According to the alcoholicity, a wine can be defined as:

- **Light (0-2).** It is said of a wine in which no pseudo-caloric sensation is perceived due to the low alcoholic content (4-7% vol).

- **Not very warm (2-4).** It is said of a wine in which a modest pseudo-caloric sensation is perceived due to the moderate alcoholic content (7.5-10.5% vol).

- **Quite warm (4-6).** It is said of a wine in which a pleasant pseudo-caloric sensation is perceived due to the moderate alcoholic content (11-12% vol).

- **Hot (6-8).** It is said of a wine in which a strong pseudo-caloric sensation is perceived due to the high alcoholic content (12.5-14.5% vol).

- **Alcoholic (8-10).** It is said of a wine in which a strong and predominant pseudo-caloric sensation is perceived due to the particularly high alcoholic content (15-18% vol), especially in some wines such as passito and liqueur.

SOFTNESS

The softness is a pleasant tactile sensation felt throughout the oral cavity as "an enveloping roundness", mainly due to the presence of glycerine (polyalcohol) in the wine, but also of ethyl alcohol and other alcohols and polyalcohols, eventual sugars, gums and mucilage.

According to the softness, a wine can be defined as:

- **Edgy (0-2).** It is said of a wine in which a clear lack of softness is not perceived. The wine in the mouth is elusive and leaves a sense of "sharpness".

- **Not very soft (2-4).** It is said of a wine in which a low sensation of softness is perceived. Normally these are young or even immature and poorly structured wines.

- **Quite soft (4-6).** It is said of a wine in which a pleasant sensation of softness is perceived. Normally these are young, ready and medium-structured wines.

- **Soft (6-8).** It is said of a wine in which a definite sensation of softness is perceived. Normally these are mature and structured wines.

- **Pasty (8-10).** It is said of a wine in which a predominant, almost excessive sensation of softness is perceived. Normally these are great white dessert wines (withering, development on the grapes of noble rot).

ACIDITY

The acidity is a gustative sensation that's due to the presence of acids in the wine and can be perceived at different levels depending on their quantity, type and penetration strength. It is perceived as a sensation of **"freshness"** more or less accentuated in the lateral areas of the tongue and sublingual, which is manifested by fluid salivation.

According to the acidity, a wine can be defined as:

- **Flat (0-2).** It is said of a wine that leaves no trace of freshness in the mouth. Normally these are old wines or those suffering from diseases.

- **Slightly cool (2-4).** It is said of a wine in which a poor but pleasant sensation of acidity is perceived, which gives a very slight salivation. Normally these are mature wines, more or less aged.

- **Quite cool (4-6).** It is said of a wine in which a discreet and pleasant sensation of acidity is perceived, which provides good salivation. Normally these are young red wines, white wines and less rosé wines.

- **Fresh (6-8).** It is said of a wine in which a strong sensation of acidity is perceived which gives an abundant salivation. Normally these are sparkling white and rosé wines and dry sparkling wines.

- **Acidulous (8-10).** It is said of a wine in which a strong and predominant sensation of acidity is perceived which gives an abundant and fluid salivation. Normally these are wines made from grapes that are not very ripe or have strong acidity.

TANNICITY

The tannicity or astringency is a tactile sensation of dryness and roughness that is perceived at the level of the entire oral mucosa and on the surface of the tongue (medial area). Associated with the sensation of astringency, it's sometimes possible to perceive a bitter vein, which can remain more or less long in the mouth depending on the type of wine in question.

According to the tannicity, a wine can be defined as:

- **Soft (0-2).** It is said of a wine in which a clear sensation of "weakness" is perceived, due to a minimal presence of tannins. Normally these are old wines or those affected by alterations.

- **Not very tannic (2-4).** It is said of a wine in which a very slight astringent sensation is perceived. Normally these are red wines that are not very structured, or aged and therefore contain the so-called "noble tannins".

- **Quite tannic (4-6).** It is said of a wine in which a sufficient and pleasant sensation of astringency is perceived. Normally these are medium to large red wines, which have already undergone a good refinement.

- **Tannic (6-8).** It is said of a wine in which a clear sensation of astringency is perceived. Normally these are young red wines or wines for which further aging is expected.

- **Astringent (8-10).** It is said of a wine in which a strong and predominant sensation of roughness and dryness is perceived. Normally these are wines with a high content of tannins, such as to represent an anomalous situation.

SAPIDITY

The sapidity is a gustative sensation due to the presence of minerals, anions and wine cations. It is perceived as a sensation of salinity more or less accentuated in the lateral and dorsal areas of the tongue, also depending on the quantity and type of acids present.

According to the sapidity, a wine can be defined as:

- **Prosy (0-2).** It is said of a wine in which no mineral sensation is perceived. Normally these are wines that are not well-worked or so old that they lack flavour.

- **Not very savory (2-4).** It is said of a wine in which a low mineral sensation is perceived. Normally these are wines with a low percentage of extractive and mineral substances or in which the sapidity is masked by acidity.

- **Quite tasty (4-6).** It is said of a wine in which a pleasant mineral sensation is perceived. Normally these are wines with an adequate percentage of extractive and mineral substances.

- **Savory (6-8).** It is said of a wine in which a very light and pleasant mineral sensation is perceived. Normally these are structured wines or in which the covering action of acids is lacking.

- **Salty (8-10).** It is said of a wine in which a predominant saline-mineral sensation is perceived. Usually these are particular wines, obtained from grapes coming from brackish areas.

STRUCTURE OR BODY OF THE WINE

The structure or body of the wine is the characteristic that depends on the amount of dry extract present, that is of all the non-volatile substances. It is greater for red wines, above all complex and for aging, compared to rose and white wines.

According to the structure or body, a wine can be defined as:

- **Thin (0-2).** It is said of a wine in which the structure is abnormal or insufficient. Normally these are wines that are not well processed or made from unhealthy grapes.

- **Weak (2-4).** It is said of a wine in which there is a modest structure due to a low quantity of gustatory elements. Normally these are wines that must be drunk young.

- **Full-bodied (4-6).** It is said of a wine in which a good and balanced structure is found. Normally these are wines made from perfectly ripe grapes.

- **Strong (6-8).** It is said of a wine in which there is a strong and balanced structure due to the wealth of gustatory elements. Normally these are great wines or wines obtained from particular processing (withering, development on noble mold grapes).

- **Heavy (8-10).** It is said of a wine in which there is an excessive and disproportionate structure that causes gustatory fatigue. Normally these are not well worked or immature wines that must be subjected to long aging.

FOOD-WINE MATCHING AIS METHOD

1. PRINCIPLE OF CONTRAPOSITION

The sapidity, the bitter tendency and the acid tendency can be considered sensations of hardness, the perception of which tends to present itself with notes of "aggressiveness" more or less accentuated. The wine in combination must have opposite characteristics of softness, able to attenuate and dampen these sensations. If the wine chosen in combination presents acidity / sapidity characteristics or a marked bitter note, it would result in an unpleasant strengthening of the sensations perceived in the food with the consequent result of an absolutely incoherent combination.

Greasiness is a tactile sensation that is perceived with a sense of slipperiness throughout the oral cavity, due to the formation of a kind of fluid film determined in particular by the oils.
The wine must have characteristics that counteract this sensation and therefore must have good tannins.
The tannins are able to determine a certain roughness in the mouth, thanks to their action of blocking the salivation.
If the preparation is also structured, perhaps obtained with red meat subjected to long cooking, we will move towards full-bodied red wines, more or less aged and more or less tannic depending on the
level of perceived oiliness.

Succulence is a tactile sensation felt due to the presence of liquids or juices present in the oral cavity.
The wine in combination must have characteristics that tend to dehydrate, to dry the liquid present. Wine alcohols and above all ethyl alcohol, are the components that show most of this dehydrating property.
It is not always necessary to match a wine with high alcohol content if the food has perceptible succulence, as long as the wine has a good tannin content.
The sweet tendency is a sensation of softness of food, which is perceived in a pleasant way and to which must correspond, always according to the principle of contrast, characteristics of acidity, therefore of freshness, and possible sapidity or effervescence of the wine proposed in combination.
The sensation of sweet tendency of food is perceived as a pleasant roundness in the mouth and therefore requires a feeling of hardness of the wine, able to determine salivation or slight pungency, which contrasts the velvety softness of this sensation.

Fatness is a tactile sensation perceived as a gustatory sensation but at the level of the entire oral mucosa and is felt as a kind of veneer in the mouth, especially on the tongue. Foods / preparations characterized by fatness often give sensations of softness that are perceived as a slight sweet tendency, and therefore the wine in combination must have characteristics of hardness, such as acidity, and possibly

sapidity and effervescence.
The acidity / sapidity of the wine cause a salivating effect and therefore tend to "partially emulsify" the fats, resulting in their "dilution".
Even the effervescence, with its characteristic of "pungency" has a certain "degreasing" property, able to clean the surface of the tongue and of the entire oral cavity.
The effervescence and acidity show a synergistic action, as the presence of carbon dioxide accentuates the sensation of freshness given by the wine, while between acidity and sapidity a masking or synergistic action may be present depending on the case.

2. PRINCIPLE OF CONCORDANCE

The sensation of sweetness is present in confectionery preparations and therefore in most desserts.
In this case the principle of contrast cannot be applied, since this sensation requires that the wine also has adequate characteristics of sweetness.
In the case of confectionery preparations, it should also be emphasized that the choice of the paired wine is conditioned not only by the level of perceptibility of the sensation of sweetness, but also by the structure of the dessert, by its consistency, by the different presence of fatty substances, of fresh fruit, dried or spice.

Aromaticity and spiciness, which at times characterize a preparation in a decisive way, are sensations that are perceived on a gustatory level but, sometimes, above all on a taste-olfactory level.
It is therefore advisable that the paired wine has a good olfactory intensity, so that the aromas that are released from the meal and the glass can be mutually enhanced, without a clear prevalence of one over the other.
The evaluation of the olfactory taste persistence of a preparation requires an adequate taste-olfactive persistence of the wine (IAP) to avoid that, as soon as the mouthful of food and the sip of wine are swallowed, not only the sensations of the one and the of the other but, on the contrary, they can be perceived in a "proportional" way.
The structure of food is given by the variety, complexity and richness of the ingredients used in the preparation. Structured and complex preparations must be combined with wines with good body, rich in components that balance those present in the meal, thus obtaining a harmonious combination.

EXAMPLES OF FOOD-WINE MATCHING ACCORDINGO TO THE CONTRAPOSITION

Dish: Rice and Luganega
Ingredients: Luganega sausage, degreased broth, grana padano, butter.
Sensorial analysis: Rice and Luganega, it is a gastronomic preparation characterized by fairly perceptible aromatic notes, medium succulence, moderate fatness, slight greasiness, good taste, tendentially sweet and of medium structure. In combination it is preferable to have a dry red wine, intense in aromas, warm in alcohol, medium soft, fairly fresh in acidity, not tannic, sapid, full-bodied.
Matching wines: Piave Merlot (Veneto), Colli di Parma Rosso (Emilia Romagna), Teroldego Rotaliano (Trentino Alto Adige).

Dish: Veal Carpaccio with Truffle and Parmesan Ingredients: Fillet of White Central Apennine Beef, White Truffle, Squeezed Lemon, Parmesan Cut in Flakes, Salt and Pepper.
Sensorial analysis: Typical meal of central Italy with pleasing and intense aromas, averagely succulent, with a light greasiness, pleasantly tasty, little perceptible fat, good taste-olfactory persistence.
In combination it is recommended a red wine of medium aging, dry, with intense olfactory sensations, reminiscent of red fruits, warm and medium soft, slightly tannic, full-bodied and with good intense aromatic persistence (I.A.P.).
Matching wines: Colli Bolognesi Merlot (Emilia Romagna), Torgiano Rosso (Umbria), Rosso Conero (Marche).

Dish: Pennette al Piacintinu
Ingredients: Pachino tomatoes, pennette rigate, garlic, onion, extra virgin olive oil, pitted black olives, butter and Piacentinu Ennese (cheese).
Sensorial analysis: Dish characterized by persistent aromaticity, good taste, slight bitter tendency, medium fatness and perceptible succulence.
In combination it is preferable a full-bodied white wine with intense, complex aromas and fruity and floral scents, quite soft and just as fresh, savory and with a long taste-olfactory persistence.
Matching wines: County of Sclafani (Sicily), Alghero Torbato (Sardinia), San Vito di Luzzi Bianco (Calabria).

Dish: Roman lamb with mushrooms.
Ingredients for 4 servings: Abbacchio Romano, blackthorn mushrooms, garlic, parsley, chervil, salt, pepper, oil and white wine.
Sensory analysis: Aromaticity, succulence, flavour, sweet tendency and greasiness characterize the perceptible taste-olfactive sensations of this preparation, of considerable structure.
In combination it is preferable to have a red wine, full-bodied, dry, fairly fresh with acidity, warm with alcohol, medium soft and with an intense and persistent bouquet.
Matching wines: Cerveteri Rosso (Lazio), Morellino di Scansano (Tuscany), Falerno del Massico Primitivo (Campania).

EXAMPLES OF FOOD-WINE MATCHING ACCORDINGO TO THE CONCORDANCE

Dish (Sweet) Bussolano di Soresina
Ingredients: donut made from flour, butter and eggs.
Sensory analysis: Bussolano is a dessert with intense olfactory sensations, aromatic and with a sweet taste, of medium succulence and slightly fat.
In combination it is preferable a sweet or passito white wine, with equally residual sugar or even a little more, full-bodied, with intense and complex olfactory sensations, reminiscent of fruit and yellow flowers, warm and soft.
Matching wines: Moscato Passito of Oltrepò Pavese (Lombardy), Erbaluce di Caluso Passito (Piedmont), Colli Euganei Fior d'Arancio (Veneto).

Dish (Sweet): Milanese panettone
Ingredients: very soft leavened dough, eggs, butter, raisins, citron and candied orange peel.
Sensorial analysis: The Panettone gives pleasing aromatic olfactory perceptions and so much sweetness to the taste, where sultanas prevail, more or less present the fatness, of discrete succulence.
Given the festive Christmas climate, sparkling or sparkling bubbles are preferable, with a rich bouquet of fruity, floral and herbaceous aromas; sweet or sweet, fresh with acidity, quite soft.
Matching wines: Moscato di Scanzo (Lombardy), Moscato d'Asti (Piedmont), Colli Piacentini Malvasia Sweet sparkling wine (Emilia Romagna).

Dish (Dessert): Neapolitan Pastiera
Ingredients: short pastry, sheep's milk ricotta, cooked wheat, sugar, lemon, cedar, orange and candied pumpkin, milk, butter, eggs, vanilla, orange blossom water, cinnamon.
Sensory analysis: the Pastiera offers pleasant aromatic olfactory perceptions; to the taste it gives so much sweetness, perceptible also the fat, the succulence and the long taste-olfactory persistence.
In combination it is preferable to have a sweet or moscato wine with a rich aromatic bouquet and fruity, floral and honey aromas; warm, soft, fresh and tasty.
Matching wines: Costa d'Amalfi Bianco Passito (Campania), Greco di Bianco Passito (Calabria), Moscato di Trani (Puglia).

Assovini.it